WITHDRAWN

imagine

being paralyzed

Linda O'Neill

The Rourke Press, Inc.
Vero Beach, Florida 32964

©2001 The Rourke Press, Inc.
All rights reserved. No part of this book may be reproduced or utilized in any form or by any means, electronic or mechanical including photocopying, recording, or by any information storage and retrieval system without permission in writing from the publisher.

NOTE: Not all of the children photographed in this book are paralyzed, but volunteered to be photographed to help raise public awareness.

PHOTO CREDITS
© Jason Marine, Inc.: cover; © Eyewire: pages 6, 9, 20; © Timothy L. Vacula: page 15; © John Harrington: page 16; © Jamie Kraslaw: page 18; © PhotoDisc: page 22; © Corel: page 25; © Access To Recreation: page 27

PRODUCED & DESIGNED by East Coast Studios
eastcoaststudios.com

EDITORIAL SERVICES
Pamela Schroeder

Library of Congress Cataloging-in-Publication Data

O'Neill, Linda
   Being Paralyzed / Linda O' Neill
   1-57103-378.5

Printed in the USA

Author's Note

This series of books is meant to enlighten and give children an awareness and sensitivity to those people who might not be just like them. We all have obstacles to overcome and challenges to meet. We need to think of the person first, not the disability. The children I interviewed for this series showed not one bit of self-pity. Their spirit and courage is admirable and inspirational.

Linda O'Neill

Table of Contents

Imagine This

You see your friends chasing after each other playing tag. You want to run and play, too. As hard as you try, though, your legs won't move. You are **paralyzed** (PAYR ah lyzd).

When you are paralyzed, you can't run, but you can do lots of other things.

Paralyzed means you can't feel or move some part of your body. There are many reasons why people are paralyzed. You may be born that way. You may be hurt in sports or a car accident. You may get very sick. If you are paralyzed, you can't run and play with your friends. However, you can do most other things they can do.

A friend lends a hand on an outdoor stroll.

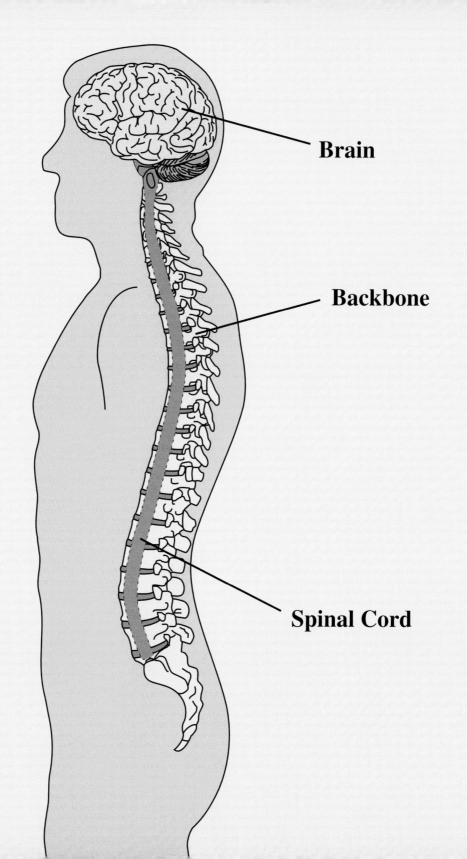

Brain

Backbone

Spinal Cord

The Message Center

Your spinal cord is a very important part of your body. It is a big bunch of nerves that carries messages to and from your brain. It runs from your head all the way down your back. Your spinal cord is the message center of your body. Your brain sends messages through your spinal cord that tell your body when to move.

Vertebrae protect your spinal cord and make up your backbone.

Each part of the spinal cord brings messages to different parts of your body. Rings of bone called **vertebrae** (VER tah brah) protect the spinal cord. These bones make up your spinal **column** (KAH lum), or backbone.

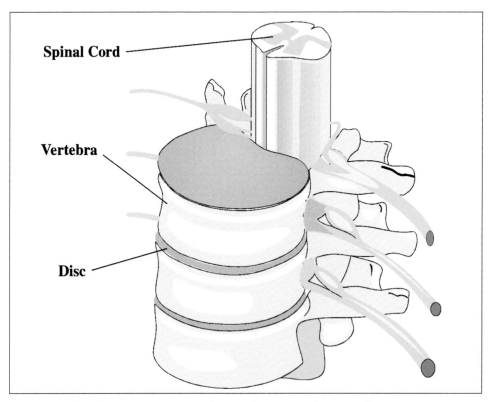

A close look at your vertebra, disc, and spinal cord.

12

Illnesses and Injuries

When your spinal cord is hurt, parts of your body can't get the messages your brain is sending. If you are born with **spina bifida** (SPY nah BIF eh dah), part of your spinal cord is not protected by your backbone. The nerves in your spine can be hurt easily. Other illnesses that can make you paralyzed are MS, which stands for **multiple sclerosis** (MULL te PULL skler OH sez), and **cerebral palsy** (sah REE brahl PAWL zee).

Injuries (IN jer eez) can paralyze people, too. Almost half of all people who hurt their spinal cords do it in car accidents. Wearing your seat belt in the car is a smart thing to do. You won't be hurt as easily with your seat belt on!

Different nerves connect to different parts of your body. If your injury is on the bottom of your spinal cord, your legs cannot send or receive messages. This is called **paraplegia** (PAYR ah PLEE gee ah). If you are hurt near the top of your neck, it is called **quadriplegia** (KWA drah PLEE gee ah). That means you cannot move your arms or legs.

It is important for everyone to attend school.

A Super Man

Christopher Reeve, the actor who played Superman in the movies, had an accident in 1995. He fell from his horse. He landed on his head and hurt his spinal cord. He was paralyzed from the neck down. He could not breathe. Now he uses a **ventilator** (VEN te LAY tor) to breathe. He has a special wheelchair, too.

Christopher Reeve travels the country giving speeches to help people with disabilities.

A super man at the movies and in real life!

Reeve did not let his injury stop him. He goes around the country giving speeches. He helps to raise money so scientists can study **disabilities** (DIS ah BILL ah teez). He also makes movies and has written a book. He has become a super man in real life!

Getting Around

The wheelchair was first made in Germany about 100 years ago. In 1932, the first modern wheelchair was built. It was light and could be folded to fit in a small space. Harry Jennings built it for his friend, Herbert Everest. Everest was paraplegic. They started a company called Everest and Jennings to **manufacture** (MAN yoo FAK chur) these wheelchairs.

Wheelchairs help people who are paralyzed. They make people **mobile** (MOW bill), or able to get around. Today there are wheelchairs that you push yourself or that someone else can push for you. You can have a wheelchair with a motor. There are even wheelchairs that have computers in them.

Some people like to push themselves. Their arms get very strong. Some people use a power chair. These chairs have motors that run on batteries. You tell the chair where to go with a joystick.

People who are quadriplegic may drive a power chair with their chins or shoulders. They may have a chair that uses "puff and sip." This means a person blows or sucks through an air tube to tell the chair where to go.

Wheelchairs help make people mobile.

Ramps and Elevators

In 1973 a new law was passed in the United States. It said all public buildings had to make it easy for disabled people to get inside. That meant adding many elevators and ramps. People in wheelchairs can't use stairs. Now lots of places have ramps. Movie theatres have special places for disabled people to park their wheelchairs. See how many buildings with ramps you can see. You may find a ramp at your school or library. Ramps are not only for people in wheelchairs. It is easier for anyone to walk up a ramp than to climb stairs.

Ramps make it easy to get into buildings.

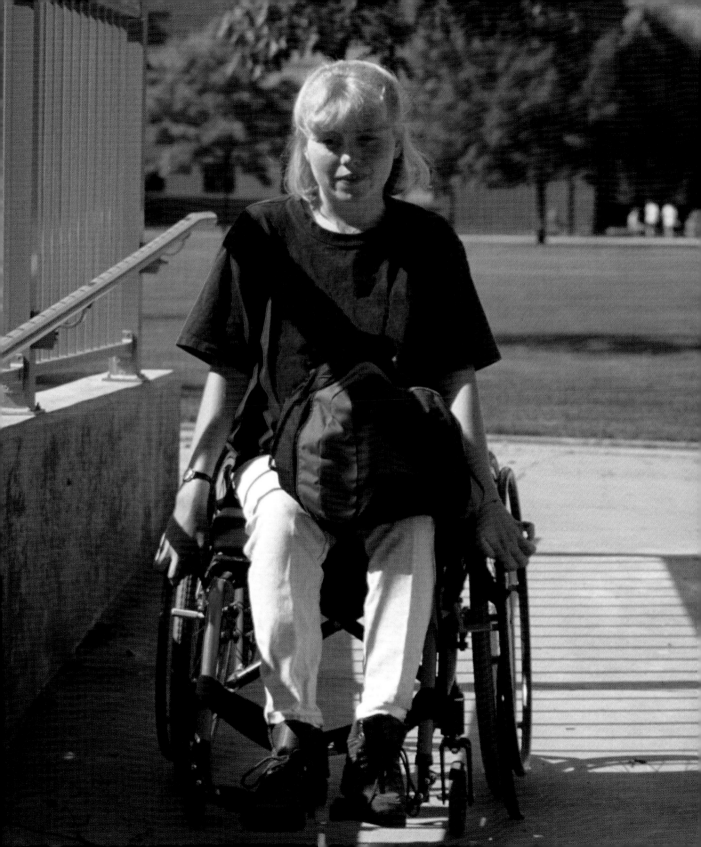

Sports

Wheelchair sports have become very popular. There are many sports you can play from a wheelchair. You can enter a **marathon** (MAYR ah thon) with your wheelchair. Boston, Massachusetts, has the world's oldest marathon. Every year people in wheelchairs enter the race. In 1999, everyone in a wheelchair who began the marathon finished the race! A lot of marathons have wheelchair racers.

You can play wheelchair basketball and hockey. You can play wheelchair tennis. You can do bodybuilding when you are older.

Swimming is something else you can do if you can move your arms. You can also scuba dive or snorkel.

Wheelchair sports are becoming very popular.

Aids

Every day new things are being made to help people who are paralyzed. There are vans made especially for people who use a wheelchair. People move up a ramp to get into the van. The van has special places for wheelchairs so they don't slide when the van is moving. When you are old enough to drive a car, there are cars you can drive with only your hands.

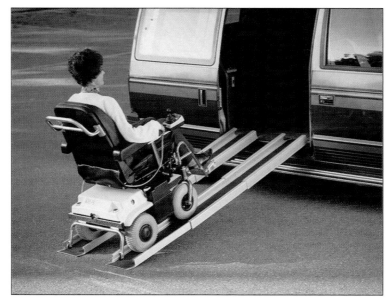

Some vans are made especially for wheelchair users.

Computers help a lot, too. Some computers learn to know your voice. It will type what you say.

If you were in a wheelchair, what new tool would you like to see?

Helping Others

You can help people who are in a wheelchair by holding doors open for them. You can ask if they need your help doing something. Remember, though, that like you, most people like to do things for themselves.

Being paralyzed means you cannot move some parts of your body. It doesn't mean you can't play sports, do well in school, or have lots of friends.

Meet Someone Special!

Meet Sam

Hi Sam, what kind of mobility problem do you have?
"I'm paraplegic. I was in a car accident with my family when I was 4."

So you've been in a wheelchair since then?
"Well, I was in the hospital a long time and when I came home, we got a wheelchair. This is a different one than I had at 4."

So you go to public school?
"Yes, I like being with all my friends."

What would you like other kids to know about you?
"That I like the same things they do and I feel the same as they do, you know."

Glossary

cerebral palsy (sah REE brahl PAWL zee) — a sickness that makes it hard to move

column (KAH lum) — an up and down row

disabilities (DIS ah BILL ah teez) — unable to do some things

injury (IN jer ee) — hurt or damage

manufacture (MAN yoo FAK chur) — to make or build

marathon (MAYR ah thon) — a 26-mile (42-km) race

mobile (MOW bill) — able to move or be moved

MS-*stands for multiple sclerosis* (MULL te PULL skler OH sez) — a disease that hurts your muscles

paralyzed (PAYR ah lyzd) — not able to move

paraplegia (PAYR ah PLEE gee ah) — paralysis of both legs

quadraplegia (KWA drah PLEE gee ah) — paralysis from the neck down

spina bifida (SPY nah BIF eh dah) — a birth defect that leaves an opening in the spinal column

ventilator (VEN te LAY tor) — a machine to help someone breathe

vertebra (VER tah brah) — one of the bones of the spinal column

Further Reading

Roy, Ron. *Move Over, Wheelchairs Coming Through.* Clarion Books, New York, 1985

Visit these Websites
www.paralysis.org

Index